HURRICANES AND TORNADOES

Louise and Richard Spilsbury

WAYLAND

First published in 2007 by Wayland

This paperback edition published in 2010 by Wayland

Copyright © Wayland 2007

Wayland,
Hachette Children's Books
338 Euston Road,
London NW1 3BH

Wayland Australia
Level 17/207 Kent Street
Sydney, NSW 2000

Editor: Susie Brooks
Managing editor: Rasha Elsaeed
Designer: Tim Mayer
Picture researcher: Shelley Noronha

British Library Cataloguing in Publication Data
Spilsbury, Louise
    Hurricanes and tornadoes. - (Natural Disasters)
    1. Hurricanes - Juvenile literature 2. Tornadoes - Juvenile
    literature
    I. Title II. Spilsbury, Richard, 1963-
    551.5'52

ISBN 9780750263535

Printed in China

Wayland is a division of Hachette Children's Books, an
Hachette UK company.
www.hachette.co.uk

Photo credits: Cover, 6 ©Jim Zuckerman/Corbis;
Bckgd 2-45 ©D.K. Demcheck/USGS; 1, 44 ©Jim
Reed/Corbis; 4 ©Reuters/Corbis; 5 ©Corbis; 7
©Reuters/Corbis; 9 ©Jim Reed/Science Photo Library; 11,
12, 13, 15 ©Pavel Rahman/ AP/PA Photos; 16
©Sygma/Corbis; 18, 19 ©Bisson Bernard/ Corbis Sygma; 20-
21 ©AFP/Getty Images; 22-23 ©Paul Hellstern/AP/PA Photos;
24 ©Corbis Sygma; 25 ©LM Otero/ AP/PA Photos; 27 ©Chris
Rimel/AP/PA Photos; 28-29 ©Rui Vieira/PA/PA Archives/PA
Photos; 30 ©newsteam.co.uk/ Simon Hadley; 31
©newsteam.co.uk/Trevor Roberts; 32-33 ©Skyscan/Corbis;
34-35 ©Noaa/Corbis; 36-37 ©Smiley N. Pool/Dallas Morning
News/Corbis; 38 ©David J. Phillip/ Pool/Reuters/Corbis; 39
©SHANNON STAPLETON/ Reuters/Corbis; 40 ©David J.
Phillip/epa/Corbis; 41 ©Benjamin Lowy/Corbis; 42-43 ©Rick
Wilking/Reuters/ Corbis; 45 ©Zul Mukhida

CONTENTS

What is a hurricane?

Hurricanes are incredibly powerful storms – the strongest and most dangerous on Earth. Hurricanes develop over warm tropical seas. Some weaken and die out over water, but others blow towards land at high speeds. Hurricanes bring violent winds that can blow down buildings and rip up trees, as well as torrential rains that can cause heavy floods. They may last for days, or even weeks, and in the past hurricanes have killed many thousands of people.

Stormy air

Hurricanes start when thunderstorm clouds drift over tropical ocean water, which is at a temperature of 26.5°C or warmer. As the air above the sea warms up, it also absorbs moisture and rises. As it rises, it cools and the moisture condenses (turns to liquid). This releases heat energy. Warm air from above the sea continues to rise and moves higher and higher and faster and faster. Gradually the air starts to whirl around.

Hurricane winds can be so powerful that they pick up and toss around objects as heavy as houses as if they were toys!

Whirling winds

At first, this type of weather system is called a tropical depression. If the winds increase to 25 kph, it becomes known as a tropical storm. After a day or two, a spiralling set of winds may reach speeds of 120 kph, and then it is defined as a hurricane. When hurricanes pass over land, the storms no longer have warm water to power them and they usually die out within a few days.

A hurricane's eye

The eye of a hurricane is in the centre of the spiralling wind. The eye is the area where the cooler air is slowly sinking. When the eye of a hurricane passes over a place, the wind there is just a gentle breeze and the rain stops. Then suddenly the rest of the hurricane passes over and the wind becomes fierce again. The eyewall is the area around the eye, where the wind and rain are strongest.

Hurricane names

Scientists give hurricanes names, so that sailors and the general public can identify them quickly. The names are created in alphabetical order and alternate between a boy's and a girl's name (the initials Q, U, X, Y, Z are not used as there are very few names that start with these letters). The largest or most destructive hurricanes can have their name retired, so that no more hurricanes are given the same name. This avoids confusion when people talk about that particular storm. Both Mitch and Katrina (featured in this book) have been retired.

GIGANTIC SIZE

Hurricanes can be enormous – the largest can be as big as 1,000 kilometres across, while others are only a few hundred kilometres wide.

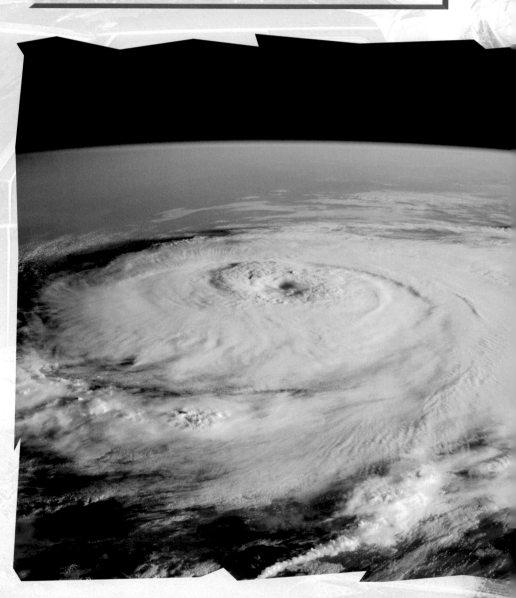

In this satellite picture you can clearly see the spiralling shape, and the eye, of a hurricane storm above Earth.

What is a tornado?

Like a hurricane, a tornado is a fast-moving, spinning funnel of air that extends from a thunderstorm to the ground. Although hurricanes and tornadoes both have spinning winds, they are very different. For one thing, tornadoes are smaller and two to six times faster than most hurricanes. And while a hurricane is a storm in itself, tornadoes usually come from a thunderstorm or even from a hurricane. Another difference is where they form. Whereas hurricanes start over water, most tornadoes form far inland, away from the sea. A tornado usually lasts less than 30 minutes, while a hurricane can go on for weeks.

Twisters!

Tornadoes look like dark, twisting columns of air that reach the ground from a cloud, which is why they are often called 'twisters'. Most tornadoes are small and last only for a few seconds. Others are large and hundreds of metres wide. Their powerful, spinning winds can suck up vehicles, trees, trains and even houses and drop them down kilometres away!

Tornadoes are often called twisters, whirlwinds, devil's tails, dust devils or willy-willys. This one is striking a farm in the USA.

How do tornadoes form?

Tornadoes form when the updraft caused by thunderstorm clouds meets certain winds. An updraft is a current of warm, moist air that rises up through a thunderstorm. When the updraft of warm, wet winds meets cold, dry winds, the cold winds are dragged down and the updraft rises faster and starts to rotate. This spinning air sucks more warm air from above the ground and moves faster and faster. The centre of a tornado is a calm eye, as in a hurricane but much narrower.

Visible winds

Like hurricanes, tornadoes are similar to spinning tops that both spiral and move backwards and forwards, left and right. The tall funnel or spout of air, reaching from high in the sky down to the ground, is visible because it contains a lot of water vapour (tiny droplets of water) and because the tornado lifts dust, dirt and other bits and pieces that spin around with its winds.

Waterspouts

A waterspout is an unusual type of tornado because it forms over rivers, lakes or oceans. While a tornado sucks up air, a waterspout also sucks up water. Most waterspouts are small, but the largest ones can be over 1,500 metres high and these can cause terrible damage to ships and boats out at sea.

A twister can turn a car park into a scrap heap within minutes.

RAINING FISH AND FROGS!

Tornadoes suck up and drop all kinds of unexpected things. They have rained down fish and toads in places as far apart as Mexico and France, and even dropped tadpoles over parts of New York, USA!

The fastest winds on Earth

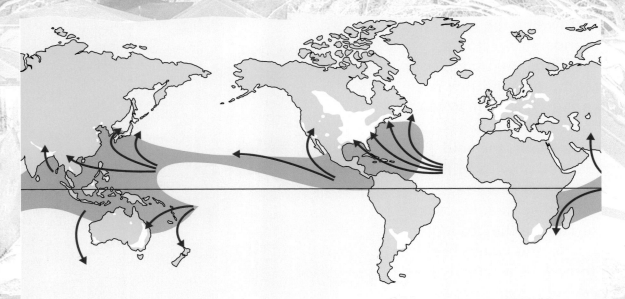

The winds within tornadoes and hurricanes can reach terrifying speeds. Scientists estimate that tornado winds can spin at up to 500 kph and hurricane winds can reach 350 kph. Tornadoes can whirl across land at up to 110 kph. The average speed a hurricane travels at is about 10 kph. However, it is very hard to measure the wind speeds inside one of these storms accurately, because measuring equipment sent into them is usually destroyed.

The dark blue areas on this map show the parts of the world where hurricanes most often develop, while the arrows show the paths they usually follow. Tornado hotspots are shaded in yellow.

Where in the world?

Tornadoes can happen almost anywhere in the world. Most strike in the USA, where there are more than 800 every year. Tornadoes also occur in Australia and many other countries, including China, India, Bangladesh, Russia, England and Germany. Hurricanes, on the other hand, start only over warm oceans so they generally happen in an area around the Equator. When hurricanes strike up in regions around the Pacific and Indian oceans they are known as typhoons or cyclones. The effects of the Coriolis Force, a force caused by the rotation of the Earth, mean that hurricanes spin anticlockwise and cyclones and typhoons spin clockwise.

When they happen

Hurricanes form only at certain times of year, known as hurricane seasons. The hurricanes that hit North America usually occur between June and November every year. Most of those hurricanes form and develop between August and October. Tornadoes can happen at any time of year, although they are more common in the USA, for example, in spring and summer when the air is hot enough to create them. In Bangladesh, most tornadoes happen in April and most hurricanes happen between August and October.

Causing destruction

Hurricane and tornado winds create destruction directly when they blow things around, but most damage to people and property is caused by objects flying like missiles in the winds. Hurricanes and tornadoes also bring violent storms with intense rain or giant hailstones, and coastal hurricanes produce wind-whipped storm waves that can tear off anything in their path and carry it along with them.

TORNADO POWER

In 1971 Theodore Fujita, a meteorology professor at the University of Chicago, invented a way of linking the damage caused by tornadoes to their wind speeds. This is known as the Fujita scale. It ranks tornado damage as light to moderate (F0 and FI), considerable to severe (F2 and F3), or devastating to incredible (F4 and F5). The weakest tornadoes (F0) may damage chimneys and signs, whereas the most violent (F5) can blow away houses.

When tornado hailstones like these hit the ground they can cause a lot of damage.

TANGAIL TORNADO, BANGLADESH, 1996

On the afternoon of 13 May 1996, a disastrous set of tornadoes ripped through the Tangail district in north-western Bangladesh, 72 kilometres north of the capital, Dhaka. The tornadoes left a path of destruction more than 1.5 kilometres wide and 80 kilometres long. At points, they sped across the ground at up to 45 kph. Many people were blown long distances by the winds, including one person who was lifted up and then dropped over 1.5 kilometres away!

Tornado times

Bangladesh has more than six tornadoes every year, because the conditions in this tropical region are right for their formation. Most occur during April, May and June. Early May is the pre-monsoon (rainy) season in Bangladesh, when the air becomes very hot. When this hot air meets cold air blowing in from the nearby Himalayan mountains, tornadoes can develop. In May 1996, temperatures reached around 40°C and the tornadoes that formed were especially destructive.

Supercell strikes

Just before the Tangail tornadoes of 1996 arrived, large hailstones fell in the area, indicating that there was a band of very cold air high in the sky. The meeting of the hot and cold bands of air caused a large thunderstorm that in turn created a supercell. A supercell is a large, spinning thunderstorm that travels long distances, lasts several hours and often produces several tornadoes. Many of the strongest tornadoes develop from a supercell.

The supercell in the district of Tangail produced a total of four tornadoes. The tornadoes rated about F4 on the Fujita scale, based on the fact that large, healthy trees over 20 metres tall were uprooted, a concrete school building collapsed and trees were stripped of their bark.

TORNADO LOSSES

- More than 1,000 deaths
- At least 37,000 people injured
- 24,000 homes damaged or destroyed

Families in Gopalpur, Bangladesh try to salvage materials from their devastated homes so that they can build themselves some sort of shelter.

TANGAIL TORNADO, BANGLADESH, 1996

A path of destruction

The 45 kph winds of the May twisters tore through 80 villages in the Tangail district of Bangladesh, destroying 17,000 houses completely and damaging 7,000 more. Trees and electricity poles were uprooted. Large fields of rice and other crops were destroyed by high winds and the following hailstorm. Huge numbers of livestock, such as chickens, cattle and goats, were killed and 80 per cent of fish ponds were also ruined. The tornadoes were so fierce that the ground was scorched and water was sucked out of wells.

Shattered houses

Many of the poor people in this area had built makeshift houses on raised banks of soil, in preparation for the rainy season when the fields become flooded. Because these houses were higher up they received the full force of the strong winds, and because they were flimsily built they were easily destroyed. People who could afford to had moved out of mud and straw huts into houses made from corrugated metal sheets. Unfortunately, the tornadoes broke these up and tossed the pieces around in the air like deadly missiles, causing many serious cuts and other injuries.

In addition, the tornadoes brought heavy rains, causing floods that washed away or submerged the homes of many poor families. This increased the number of people left without shelter.

A woman and her three children try to reach shelter on a banana raft. Their home was among tens of thousands destroyed by the tornadoes' winds and rains.

Individuals and injuries

Some people were buried alive under buildings shattered by the storm. For example, in the village of Bashail 120 people were killed, many of whom were students who were crushed when their school building was blown down. Others drowned in the floods that followed. But most of the people who died were killed by flying objects, such as tree branches and pieces of metal. In Pabna, a local man counted 65 dead bodies suspended in trees.

Hospital pressures

Local hospitals were too small to take many patients. For example, one hospital designed to treat 35 patients suddenly had 2,000 casualties at its doors. Many of the injured people had no choice but to walk or be carried to the Tangail General Hospital. Here, beds soon filled up and more than 1,000 patients had to lie on the floor. The electricity was down, so no operations could be done and the more serious cases were sent to Dhaka. Most people waited over a day before being seen by a doctor. This delay proved fatal. Many of the badly injured victims and the weak or elderly died from loss of blood or because their wounds became infected.

The Tangail tornadoes injured so many people that hospitals ran out of beds and did not have enough staff to treat victims promptly.

TANGAIL TORNADO, BANGLADESH, 1996

Rescue and relief

Around 24 hours after the disaster, the Bangladesh government sent rescue workers. Soldiers, army medical teams and a rescue and relief force arrived, as did workers from groups such as the Red Cross. Rescuers and volunteers searched for survivors, and soldiers cleared rubble and buried dead bodies. Other workers helped relatives and friends look for missing loved ones. Unfortunately, rescue efforts were hampered by the flooded roads and continuing heavy rainfall, which meant that trucks could not get through. There were also difficulties with communications because telephone lines were down.

Shelter and sanitation

Two of the most important priorities were to provide shelter and sanitation. People's homes had been destroyed and at night survivors were sleeping in the open under torrential rains. The approaching monsoon season meant that the conditions would only get worse. The monsoon is a seasonal wind that brings relentless, very heavy rains to countries such as India and Bangladesh every year from the middle of May to October. Although there was ample rainfall coming, fresh water was in short supply after the tornadoes because many of the wells that used to provide water had been ripped out by the storm, and many other water supplies had been polluted by mud and dirt.

The government supplied building materials, such as reused metal and plastic sheets, so that people could make shelters. And the Bangladesh Government Health Engineering department made rebuilding damaged drinking wells and toilet facilities a priority – many were repaired within a week. Government workers also gave out lentils, rice, cooking oil and other foodstuffs, as well as medicines and first aid kits, bedding and clothing.

FUTURE FATE?

The people in the Tangail area are very religious. Many considered the tornadoes to be acts of God and accepted the disaster as fate. If people believe there is nothing they can do because tornadoes are God's punishment, they may avoid taking action to reduce risks in future.

Live and learn?

At the time of the 1996 disaster, there were no warning systems or preparedness programmes for tornadoes in place in Bangladesh. People had no idea how to react when faced with a tornado and there were no shelters for them to escape to. By 2004, when another tornado hit a different area of Bangladesh and killed 111 people, there was still no formal warning system in place. As at Tangail, in 2004 many people were killed by flying metal from tin houses. The problem is that less economically developed countries (LEDCs) such as Bangladesh often cannot afford to make the changes necessary to protect their inhabitants.

Survivors queued for a long time to collect precious food rations from government officials. Soldiers were on hand to ensure people waited their turn, however desperate they were.

HURRICANE MITCH, CENTRAL AMERICA, 1998

From 26 October to 1 November 1998, Hurricane Mitch wreaked havoc across parts of Central America. It was the worst hurricane to hit the region for over 200 years. More than 9,200 people were killed and over 9,000 remain missing, presumed dead, making Mitch one of the deadliest hurricanes ever recorded.

This satellite image shows Hurricane Mitch swirling over the Caribbean Sea towards Honduras, Belize and Guatemala.

Mexico

Belize

Guatemala

Honduras

HURRICANE POWER

Hurricanes vary in size and strength, so scientists have devised a way to categorize them to give people a clearer idea of what should be expected in a coming storm. This measurement is called the Saffir-Simpson scale. It ranks hurricanes from 1 (least dangerous) to 5 (extremely dangerous).

Path of destruction

As Hurricane Mitch moved through Central America, it dropped as much as 2 metres of rain on some regions, causing terrible flooding and landslides. The heavy, continuous rains caused at least 50 rivers to overspill their banks. Subsequent floods swept away bridges and roads and destroyed many towns including Tegucigalpa, the capital of Honduras. The worst affected areas were Honduras and Nicaragua, but Mitch also had an impact on people in parts of Guatemala, El Salvador, Belize, Costa Rica and Mexico.

Hurricane strength

Hurricane Mitch formed over the Caribbean Sea and increased rapidly in size and force as it drifted across the very warm water there. The hurricane rated 5 on the Saffir-Simpson scale – meaning it was extremely dangerous – for more than 33 hours. Some of its winds raged at speeds of over 180 kph and lasted for more than 15 hours.

DISASTER DAYS

24 OCTOBER 1998
am Hurricane Mitch forms over the sea south of Jamaica.

pm Mitch is 160 kilometres from the coast of Jamaica.

25 OCTOBER
Heavy rainfall causes flooding in the Cayman Islands.

26 OCTOBER
Mitch reaches its peak with wind speeds of 290 kph.

27-28 OCTOBER
Mitch heads towards Central America.

29 OCTOBER
Mitch moves towards Honduras and weakens to a tropical storm.

30-31 OCTOBER
Mitch drops torrential rains over Honduras, Nicaragua and some neighbouring countries, causing devastating floods.

1 NOVEMBER
Mitch breaks up over Guatemala.

OCTOBER 1999
Thousands of people are still living in shelters; aid workers continue to provide food, water and sanitation and work to improve healthcare services.

OCTOBER 2003
Life is back to normal; people are back at school and work; communities have been rebuilt; replanted trees and crops are growing well; many areas have alarm systems in place in case of similar disasters in the future.

HURRICANE MITCH, CENTRAL AMERICA, 1998

Storm impact

Most of the people who died as a result of Hurricane Mitch drowned in the floods it created. Hurricane Mitch dropped a huge volume of rain, particularly over Nicaragua and Honduras, and this caused widespread flooding when rivers overflowed their banks. Floods were also caused by a storm surge. This is when hurricane winds create high waves that can force their way up rivers and cause the rivers to burst their banks. In Nicaragua, 500 drowned bodies were found in one river alone. In the Caribbean Sea, the hurricane caused 15-metre high waves and winds of 160 kph that battered and sank a sailing ship and its 31-man crew.

Landslides

The heavy rain also caused landslides (the sudden slipping down of large amounts of mud and soil). In Honduras, about 25 small villages were destroyed by landslides. On Friday 3 October the crater lake at the top of the Casita volcano overflowed and the walls of the volcano collapsed. This created a terrible mudslide that slipped down and buried an area 16 kilometres long and 8 kilometres wide, killing 2,000 people.

Honduras was the country most affected by the hurricane. This photo shows damage in the capital, Tegucigalpa, which had to be rebuilt after the storm.

HURRICANE COSTS

- 18,200 presumed dead
- 13,000 people injured
- 1.5 million people made homeless
- 500,000 people in shelters

Mudslides caused terrible scenes of devastation in Honduras, leaving people struggling to retrieve their property. The president of Honduras, Carlos Flores Facusse, claimed the storm destroyed 50 years of progress.

Extent of the damage

The flooding and mudslides damaged or destroyed tens of thousands of homes, most of which were in Honduras and Nicaragua, as well as schools, clinics and hospitals. Flooding also ruined farmland and food stores. Large areas of crops were destroyed, including valuable export crops such as bananas, sugar cane and coffee. Huge numbers of farm animals, such as cattle, were killed and the shrimp farm industry was badly affected when shrimp ponds were flooded with dirty water and mud. Around 70-80 per cent of the transport infrastructure, such as roads and bridges, was wiped out. In fact, the damage was so severe that existing maps became useless.

Did poverty make matters worse?

Many people believe that the number of deaths would not have been so high if the area had not been so poor. The flooding in Nicaragua was made worse because the trees on many hillsides had been cut down for logging, farming and houses. Many poor people lived on these hillsides in makeshift homes. The heavy rains and mudslides raced down the bare slopes at great speeds and swept away everything in their path.

EYEWITNESS

❝ The mud was as high as the treetops. It tore down the trees and the houses. The place is a desert now. There's nothing to be seen. ❞

Rosa Cabellero, who survived a mudslide in Honduras that wiped out four communities

HURRICANE MITCH, CENTRAL AMERICA, 1998

In need of aid

People in Nicaragua, Honduras and other places affected by Hurricane Mitch needed urgent assistance. In Honduras, for example, a fifth of the country's population – up to 1.5 million people – had been left homeless. And in the damp heat of this tropical environment, fatal diseases such as cholera soon spread among survivors who had no other choice but to drink water polluted by dirt and dead bodies. In response to the disaster, countries as far away as Japan, the UK and Russia donated over US$6 billion in aid.

First response

Charitable organizations such as Oxfam and the Red Cross sent aid workers to the area almost immediately. They provided people with food, clean water, medical treatment and shelters. Helicopters were used to rescue survivors who were left clinging to rooftops, and to take supplies to areas cut off by floods, but these aircraft were in short supply. Teams of specialists also helped to reunite people with loved ones who had been lost in the storms. Bulldozers were brought in to try to clear roads.

Recovering farmland

In this extremely poor part of the world, aid from international organizations was vital. In Honduras, 80 per cent of the banana crop was destroyed. Coffee, bean, sugar and banana crops were ruined in other countries too, including Nicaragua, El Salvador and Costa Rica. Aid organizations provided farm workers with new plants and farm tools so they could earn a living again. Unfortunately, floods washed away the fertile top layer of soil from whole plantations and covered others with sand, so some farmland was lost for ever.

Gradually new fruit trees, such as these banana saplings, were planted and farming communities in the region began to rebuild their shattered lives.

Rebuilding homes

Building new homes was another important part of long-term recovery. One of the reasons homes had been so easily destroyed by Hurricane Mitch was that they were flimsy, so aid organizations worked to help people build stronger homes for the future. However, the number made homeless was so large that this problem has still not been completely solved and some people continue to live in potentially dangerous sites on hillsides.

OKLAHOMA TWISTERS, USA, 1999

Tornadoes can be deadliest when they occur in groups, known as tornado swarms. In May 1999, a swarm of around 70 tornadoes struck a total of five US states, from Texas to South Dakota. Winds in some of these tornadoes blew at speeds of over 300 kph and some tornadoes measured more than 1.5 kilometres wide. What made the swarm so deadly was that it struck towns and cities with high populations.

Tornado Alley

Tornadoes occur in this region of the USA every year, to the extent that the wide, flat expanse of land between the Rocky Mountains and the Mississippi River is known as Tornado Alley. Cool, dry air moving in from Canada gets diverted towards the east by the Rockies. Over the Great Plains, it clashes with moist, warm air from the Gulf of Mexico and this often creates the huge storm clouds that can generate tornadoes.

Weather alert

Weather forecasters were on alert in May 1999. Conditions were ripe for tornadoes, with cold air from the west clashing with warm, moist air coming from the east. Unlike hurricanes, tornadoes form suddenly and extra staff had been called in to meteorological offices to keep an eye on the situation and to spot a tornado as soon as it formed.

Tornado Watch

By late afternoon, fears were confirmed. At 4.45 pm meteorologists issued a Tornado Watch, warning people that tornadoes with wind speeds of up to 120 kph were possible. Two minutes later they issued the first Tornado Warning. The first twister was spotted at 4.51 pm. At 7 pm a tornado struck in Cleveland County and 25 minutes later another moved through Oklahoma City. People across the USA began hearing about the devastation in early reports. Oklahoma was by far the worst hit – 38 people died there. While most tornadoes last only briefly, the one that hit Oklahoma stayed on the ground for nearly four hours.

TORNADO COSTS

- 47 deaths
- 2,000 homes damaged or destroyed
- Cost of damage: US$500 million

The twisters of May 1999 blackened the skies for hours. The biggest rated F5 on the Fujita scale.

OKLAHOMA TWISTERS, USA, 1999

EYEWITNESS

❝ I heard it. I heard the popping and then I heard the trees crunching and then my house was gone. ❞

Mary Pat Faris, who weathered the storm in her bathtub

The aftermath

Tornadoes break up anything in their path and blast debris in every direction and at high speeds. In May 1999, the swarm of tornadoes that hit Oklahoma peeled off the top layer of pavements and ripped houses from their foundations. Trees and plants were swept away, leaving expanses of dirt and mud that had once been green land. The air was filled with so much debris that witnesses said they could smell sawdust. Power lines were snapped in half and vehicles were swept up, tossed around and dropped again. One car was wrenched from its owner's garage, swirled around and then dumped in a swimming pool in a neighbour's back garden!

You can see the path taken through Oklahoma City by the twisters that flattened homes as they swept down the streets.

Rescue and relief

After the tornadoes had passed through, all that remained of many streets were piles of rubble. Rescue workers arrived on the scene within hours and began searching for survivors. They used specially trained dogs to sniff out victims who were trapped under crushed buildings. Cranes and other machinery were brought in to lift away heavy sections of debris so rescuers could reach victims safely.

The skeleton of a wind-thrown vehicle is left wrapped around a tree. Can you imagine how it would feel to see your family's belongings ripped apart and tossed away like this by a tornado?

Some people who had lost their homes moved in with friends, and American Red Cross workers set up shelters for other people. Individuals offered assistance too, including a landlord who donated two houses to families who had lost their homes in the tornadoes. Aid poured in from all over the USA, in the form of money, tins of food, clothing and toiletries. And because the USA is a more economically developed country (MEDC), the government was able to provide financial assistance to help those in trouble. Extra temporary jobs were created in the area to help people earn money and get back on their feet.

Clearing up

Clearing up the debris was a major task. Crews using heavy equipment took weeks to carry truckloads of rubble and waste to a temporary dump site. The tornado created as much waste in four hours as the area usually produced in a whole year. It took over a year to rebuild the houses that had been lost, and in some places reconstruction had not been completed even after a year had passed.

OKLAHOMA TWISTERS, USA, 1999

Being prepared

This storm could have been far more deadly if it were it not for the accurate forecasts and warnings given. A tornado with wind speeds of over 300 kph can flatten practically anything in its path, so the only way to survive it is to get out of its way. To evacuate in time, people need advance warning. They also need to know what to do and where to go. In Tornado Alley, most people are aware of the risks of tornadoes, and meteorologists believe that if this tornado had happened anywhere else in the USA there would have been a much greater loss of life.

Weather warnings

The fact that people in the area were well informed made the difference between life and death for many. Weather forecasters gave continuous coverage of the storm, using information relayed to them from helicopters up in the air and radars that showed the path the tornadoes were likely to take. Crews on the helicopters even filmed the tornado so people could see exactly where the tornado was and what it was capable of. Police officers walked the streets warning residents, so everyone knew there was a danger.

EYEWITNESS

❝ It was as close to a textbook as you could get... From everything I know, what took place in Oklahoma on Monday is a model for other cities to follow. ❞

Joe Schaefer, director of the weather service's Storm Prediction Centre in Norman, Oklahoma

Tornado plans

Once a tornado warning has been given, people in Tornado Alley know that it is time to move to a safe shelter or evacuate. Many people survived because they moved into a basement or a safe shelter, such as a storm cellar. These are basements or rooms that have walls that are extra thick and strong because they have been strengthened with concrete or sheets of steel. Safe rooms are also fixed to the foundations of houses to stop them being lifted away.

Safety education

People living in regions within Tornado Alley are well prepared partly because they may have experienced tornadoes before. Another reason is education. Many local schools run a tornado awareness week before the main tornado season, in which children are taught what to do if a tornado warning is given. In addition, authorities give out leaflets explaining other ways to keep safe – for example, how people should cover themselves with mattresses and cushions to prevent injury from flying glass and debris. Knowledge like this saves lives.

Many schoolchildren within Tornado Alley are taught where to go and what to do if a tornado strikes. These children are in a special safe room, learning the best position to get into to protect themselves from flying debris.

TORNADOES IN THE UK, 2005

A small but violent tornado hit the city of Birmingham in the UK on 28 July 2005. The tornado followed a narrow, zig-zag path and left a trail of destruction across streets full of houses and a park. It caused extensive damage to buildings, gardens and vehicles. It destroyed part of a supermarket, uprooted around 1,000 trees and damaged more than 100 homes. Rows of houses were left with shattered windows and streets were littered with glass, bricks, furniture and everything from clothing to fruit and other items torn from shop windows.

EYEWITNESS

❝ There were a couple of really loud thunder claps and bright lightning strikes and then the wind picked up… there were trees and bricks flying about. It was madness; cars being lifted up; flag poles snapped off at their bases. It suddenly went weirdly quiet and then seemed to pass. ❞

Jane Trobridge, who was at work when the tornado struck

TORNADO COSTS

- 19 people injured
- 1,500 people affected
- 20 buildings destroyed
- More than 100 homes damaged
- Cost of damage: more than £40 million (US$79 million)

The tornado's progress

Around midday a line of thunderstorms stretched across the UK from mid-Wales to London. By 1 pm the storms were headed north and they were growing stronger. At 2.30 pm the storms became a tornado that hit south Birmingham. It lasted less than 10 minutes before weakening and moving northwards across the city.

Impact on people

In this tornado, 19 people were injured. Three of the victims were seriously wounded by bricks, slates and other debris that went flying through the air. A car park attendant was caught inside a wooden shed and thrown across the road by the winds, and a woman's legs were badly cut by a flying street sign. One person told of leaping from his van just moments before a tree crashed straight through his windscreen. Another witness said he had seen a mother manage to grab her baby from its pram just seconds before the pram was blown violently across the street. Some children described being lifted off their feet!

The weather that day

Witnesses said the tornado winds hit at around 2.30 pm, when the sky turned a brown-grey colour. This came soon after a sudden and torrential shower of rain. Once the winds had died down, the weather turned sunny and so warm that people changed into shorts. The violent weather was caused by the convergence, or meeting, of warm, very wet conditions heading north with colder, dry air moving in from the east. These winds went on to cause a second but much smaller tornado in Peterborough.

This aerial shot shows some of the streets damaged by the Birmingham tornado of 2005.

Rapid response

An Emergency Plan Response Team arrived in the area within 30 minutes. Medical staff treated injured victims on the spot or transported them to hospital. In one street there were so many cuts and minor injuries that paramedics set up a kind of field hospital and treated people as they came along. The other priority was to evacuate the residents in case damaged trees or buildings fell and caused more injuries. Roads in the area were closed off while emergency services used sniffer dogs to see if anyone was trapped in the rubble. Other workers checked for possible gas leaks, which could have caused fires.

Some residents were taken to emergency accommodation, for example at a local sports centre and a community centre, and some stayed with family, friends or neighbours. People who had to leave everything when they left their homes were also given supplies, such as medicines, toiletries, nappies and toys. Many pets were cared for and given temporary homes.

As is usual in tornadoes, much of the damage to Birmingham was caused by falling or flying debris. This car was crushed by a wall that was blown down by the fierce winds.

Cleaning up

When families had been evacuated, workers began to remove debris from the roofs and gutters of buildings. They then checked that the buildings were stable enough for structural engineers and building surveyors to inspect them more closely. Around 20 properties had to be demolished. Some buildings were considered dangerous and streets were closed off to prevent people returning to them to collect belongings. The authorities set up a tornado hotline, a special phone number people could call to find out whether or not it was safe for them to return home.

Highway and tree officers cleared branches and other debris from the streets. They also checked damaged trees overhanging roads to ensure that they were not about to fall. There were security officers and police on duty 24 hours a day to stop people from entering the streets and to protect empty properties against looting.

The damage to some homes was so enormous that afterwards the buildings had to be demolished and rebuilt.

The cost of repairs

Unfortunately, even in a more economically developed country such as the UK, the cost of a disaster like this can be high. Around half of the 1,500 victims of the tornado had to pay the enormous cost of house repairs themselves because they did not have insurance. The Sparkbrook area of the city, which was one of the worst hit, is one of Birmingham's poorest districts. Many of the people who live there cannot afford insurance, partly because the burglary rate is so high that the cost of insurance for the area is too expensive. Many people were left with bills for thousands of pounds covering roof and brickwork repairs, and some people had seen their entire homes being demolished.

RECORD BREAKER

This was the most costly tornado in UK history. It cost tens of millions of pounds to repair the extensive damage to property. The tornado was also one of the strongest to have been recorded in the UK for 30 years.

Counting tornadoes

The tornado in Birmingham was not an isolated event. Another tornado struck the city that October, and tornadoes also hit Coventry and London in the same year. On average, the UK experiences 35-40 tornadoes a year, but this average does vary. In 2004 there were 70 tornadoes, in 2005 there were 63 and in 2006 there were 49. Most tornado reports are from the Midlands, central-southern England, south-east England and East Anglia. Some occur in south-west England, north-west England, north-east England and Wales. Tornadoes are rare in Northern Ireland and Scotland.

Tornado capital!

You might be surprised to discover that there are more tornadoes per square kilometre each year in the UK than there are in the USA. This fact was calculated by the late Dr Fujita, creator of the Fujita scale that measures tornado strength. Fujita worked out that as the UK has an average of more than 30 tornadoes every year and is 38 times smaller than the USA, people in the UK are twice as likely to witness a tornado. The difference is, of course, that the tornadoes in the UK are much smaller than those in the USA and their effects are rarely felt, let alone reported.

BRITISH SCALE

In the UK, a scale based on the Beaufort wind scale is used to rate the intensity of a tornado. It is known as the TORRO (Tornado and Storm Research Organization) scale or T-scale and has a range from T0 to T10. The UK Meteorological Office estimated that the Birmingham tornado had a general T4 rating on this scale, with a short spell as a T5 tornado. This means that it had wind speeds of between 150 and 210 kph, which is equivalent to an F2 on the Fujita scale.

Many scientists believe that air pollution, such as the carbon dioxide released from chimneys when fossil fuels are burned, contributes to global warming and that this climate change may lead to an increase in the number of tornadoes and hurricanes in the future.

TORNADO MONTH

On 21 November 1981, 104 tornadoes whipped the UK. This is the most tornadoes to have hit any country in Europe within one day!

The future

Some scientists say that climate change will make tornadoes more common in the UK because there will be an increase in the vigorous mixing of moist, warm air and cold air that creates these storms. If the number of tornadoes increases, so might their intensity. In regions of the USA affected by tornadoes, people are aware of what to do and rely on local radio for up-to-the-minute reports and advice about storms. As yet, such a system does not exist in the UK for tornadoes and some people are asking whether people in the UK should be more prepared.

HURRICANE KATRINA, USA, 2005

Hurricane Katrina formed during the 2005 Atlantic hurricane season. It became the deadliest hurricane to hit the USA for more than 75 years. Katrina built up near the Bahamas on 23 August, hit Florida and then returned to the sea where it strengthened and doubled in size. When it crossed land on 29 August on the north central Gulf Coast, it caused devastation up to 240 kilometres inland. Around 1,850 people lost their lives in Hurricane Katrina and in the floods that it created.

This satellite image shows Hurricane Katrina approaching land in the morning of 28 August 2005.

HURRICANE COSTS

- 1,850 deaths
- More than 500,000 people made homeless
- More than 2 million people evacuated
- Cost of damage: around US$75 billion

Path of destruction

Hurricane Katrina left destruction over an area almost as big as the UK. It caused horrific loss of life and damage in the US states of Louisiana, Mississippi and Alabama. New Orleans suffered hurricane effects for hours and the flooding there caused terrible damage and loss of life. Passing on to Gulfport, the 217 kph winds crashed boats into seaside buildings. Then, in the coastal city of Biloxi, a 9-metre storm surge smashed into an apartment block and killed 30 people. Up to 90 per cent of buildings were destroyed at Biloxi and Gulfport. In Mobile, waves full of mud and sand hit the eastern shore of Mobile Bay and flooded mansions worth millions of dollars.

DISASTER DAYS

25 AUGUST 2005
Hurricane Katrina forms over the Caribbean Sea.
11.45 pm Hurricane Katrina hits Florida with wind speeds of 130 kph; nine people die.

26 AUGUST
Katrina moves into the Gulf of Mexico and gains strength over its warm waters.

26 AUGUST
Katrina's strongest winds reach 185 kph, making it a Category 3 hurricane.

28 AUGUST
Katrina becomes Category 5; people in New Orleans are told to evacuate and roads are jammed as families flee.

29 AUGUST
6.10 am After weakening to Category 4, Katrina hits New Orleans with winds of up to 200 kph and heavy rain; banks of earth called levees, built to prevent flooding, break and water floods the city.

30 AUGUST
Katrina finally weakens over Mississippi state.

AUGUST 2006
Only 200,000 of New Orleans' 500,000 original residents have returned; almost a third of schools, hospitals and libraries are still closed, as are half the city's public transport systems.

HURRICANE KATRINA, USA, 2005

New Orleans

The risk of devastation to New Orleans was well known. The city lies just off the Gulf of Mexico, where many hurricanes start. It is also built on ground that lies below sea level. Both the Mississippi River, which runs through the centre of the city, and the lake to its north are at higher levels than the city itself. These factors make New Orleans particularly vulnerable to floods. To protect the city and stop these water sources overflowing during storms, the river and the lake are kept in place by high banks of earth called levees.

EYEWITNESS

This is not a drill! It is my grave duty to order the mandatory evacuation of New Orleans and its surrounding parishes. The storm we are expecting to hit the city this afternoon is without precedent. Please get out of the city!

Mayor Nagin's radio warning to residents of New Orleans before the hurricane hit and the levees broke

WILD WINDS

Even before the floods took hold, Hurricane Katrina's winds blasted out windows from buildings and flung beds and furniture into the streets. Trees were snapped in half and power lines collapsed.

Lost levees

Unfortunately, up until August 2005, the levees were strong enough only to hold off a direct hit from a Category 3 hurricane. Katrina was a powerful Category 5, and although the centre of the hurricane did not hit the city, heavy rain and storm surges caused flooding that broke through parts of the levees. When the flood defences broke, about 80 per cent of New Orleans was filled with water.

In some streets only signposts and treetops poked above the surface of the flood water, with a trail of devastation strewn below. Roads and bridges were blocked and communications were lost. Shops and homes were wrecked, cars and other vehicles were hurled around the streets and streams of shattered glass and other debris swirled around. In total, about 78,000 homes were ruined in New Orleans.

Lost lives

In spite of evacuation warnings, many people had chosen not to leave New Orleans or had been unable to leave in time. Some were too old or too weak; others did not have a car or wanted to stay to look after their pets. When water flooded their houses, some people smashed their way into their attics and out on to their roofs using hatchets and sledge hammers. Other people had to swim for their lives or wade through deep water to escape to dry land, taking care to look out for dangerous snakes along the way. More than 700 people were drowned by the massive flooding, and survivors reported seeing dead bodies floating past them in the murky flooded streets.

In places the flood water in New Orleans was 6 metres deep, leaving only the roofs of many buildings visible above the water.

Rescue efforts

Workers organized by FEMA (the Federal Emergency Management Agency) arrived on Tuesday 30 August. Using helicopters and boats they began to pick up survivors stranded on rooftops across the area. It was very hot, there were mosquitoes everywhere, and rescuers often had to push aside drowned bodies to reach survivors in the dirty water. Injured people and the elderly or sick were evacuated, but other survivors were left at shelters such as the Superdome Stadium within the city.

The government declared a state of emergency along the Gulf Coast, in the hope of speeding up the delivery of food, water and fuel to the region. But progress was slow and by Sunday 4 September thousands of people were still stranded, waiting for help. The US government appealed for international aid including blankets, food, water trucks and first aid kits.

EYEWITNESS

❝ You're a looter when you're taking stuff you don't need. You're a survivor when you're taking stuff you need to survive. I took some sardines and canned goods... I was trying to find water. There were eight of us in the house; we had to live. ❞

Gerard Broussard, 18, flood victim

Many of the survivors who had smashed their way through attic roofs to escape the flood waters waited for days before they were rescued by helicopter.

Superdome shelter

By Wednesday 7 September, there were 26,000 people inside the Superdome – the city's only official shelter – and a similar number in the nearby convention centre. They had little food or water, and when the air-conditioning broke down conditions in the stadium were very uncomfortable. Evacuation from the Superdome began on the Wednesday, but it was very slow. Many people were desperate by this time, and angry. On the Friday food, water and medical supplies arrived, but many people were not helped out of the city until the following Monday.

Rescue workers faced many dangers, including fires, poisonous snakes, polluted water and sharp or floating debris, to find survivors.

Looting and raiding

In desperation, some people started to raid shops to get food and water. Other people became looters and took advantage of the situation by robbing abandoned shops and houses. In places, fights broke out as people argued over a share in the limited supplies of petrol and other goods. Thousands of troops and police were sent in to keep the peace and protect innocent people.

Pet rescue

More than 250,000 pets were left stranded by the storm. Many owners had left their pets with food and water because they could not take them and only expected to be away for a short time. Members of the American Society for the Prevention of Cruelty to Animals and other organizations travelled by boat or on foot through polluted flood waters to help dehydrated, starving animals. They took the pets to a safe place where they were treated by a vet and given food and water. At these shelters, volunteers helped families to search through thousands of cages to find their pets.

Rebuilding homes and lives

In the weeks after the disaster, many relief workers and volunteers were involved in trying to reunite families who had been separated when they were evacuated or in the confusion of the storm and flooding. Around 5,000 children were separated from their families, many of whom were sent away from New Orleans in buses. These children and other people were desperate to know whether their loved ones were alive and wanted to find them. Many people had their mobile phones with them when they escaped, and these were very useful in helping people to contact each other. The last displaced child was reunited with her family in March 2006, six months after the disaster.

Rebuilding plans

The work of repairing the city's levees, pumping out the flood waters and finding homes for tens of thousands of displaced residents was underway by Friday 2 September. FEMA funded rebuilding projects and programmes to help people afford new homes. They also built 40 camps for volunteers who were helping victims of the disaster, for example by clearing out the debris and cleaning up streets and homes. However, progress was slow even in this, the wealthiest country in the world, and insurance companies refused to pay to build new houses unless the levees were guaranteed to be rebuilt to a much higher standard.

Before the levees could be repaired, flood water had to be pumped out of the city via huge pipes like the ones seen here.

One year on, much of the debris left by Hurricane Katrina had still not been cleared away.
This house and car in New Orleans were left abandoned where they fell.

One year on

Katrina caused so much damage to property that it became the most expensive natural disaster in US history. Whole neighbourhoods had to move in with friends, find new homes or live in FEMA mobile homes or trailers while they waited for new housing to be built. Many of the evacuees had been living below the poverty line before the storm struck, and while the wealthier side of the city was rebuilt quite quickly, the rest was much slower to get the assistance it needed. After a year, many families were still struggling to find new jobs, homes and a return to a normal lifestyle. Many streets in New Orleans were still empty.

EYEWITNESS

❝ I'm shy and I have to start at a new school. I'm gonna have to make new friends, but then I'm gonna have to go back to New Orleans, once they flush the water out. ❞

Dedrionne McCarvy, 12, one of many children who had to go to new schools in places to which they had been evacuated

Preparation and prevention

In spite of early warning systems and early evacuation calls, Katrina was still the costliest and one of the deadliest hurricanes in US history to date. The disaster prompted the authorities to look at what went wrong and how things could be improved in the future. In practical terms, Louisiana state and other regions that rely on levees to prevent flooding are now looking at different designs for the rebuilding of levees. In terms of organization, the Katrina disaster exposed problems with leadership and communication between government departments, federal agencies and relief organizations. This led to delays that caused suffering and maybe even loss of life, so improved ways of co-ordinating responses to future disasters are also now under review.

Forward planning

It would be an enormous and expensive exercise to do a test evacuation on a whole city, so many US authorities – and those from as far away as the UK – have been looking at the evacuation response of New Orleans to learn lessons. They are examining the failure of New Orleans to equip its designated shelter (the Superdome Stadium) with supplies such as water and medical equipment. They are also asking why so many people were still in the city when the levees broke, after an evacuation order had been given. They are looking at providing adequate public transport to get people out, and planning special road routes to avoid the traffic jams that prevented so many New Orleans from escaping in time.

EYEWITNESS

❝ The first and foremost lesson we learned from the death and devastation caused by our country's most destructive natural disaster: no matter how prepared we think we are, we must work every day to improve. ❞

Frances Townsend, White House homeland security adviser

Forward planning is vital for successful evacuations, but it is very hard to test the impacts of a large-scale exodus from a city when traffic jams like this one on the road from New Orleans are likely to form.

Can Louisiana's coastal towns ever be safe?

In the past, New Orleans relied on wetlands (natural marshy areas) to absorb storm surges and inland cypress forests to slow the winds. As more and more people have come to live in the area, these natural barriers have been disappearing. Wetlands have been drained for building or farmland, and channels dug for ships have led to salt water getting into freshwater swamps and killing off the cypress trees.

Channels that have been cut out of the river bed to create quick routes for ships to get to sea also provide a direct path for the large waves created by storm surges to head straight for places where people live. That is why many people in Louisiana have been campaigning for government funding to help them restore the marshes and swamplands there.

SOME OF THE WORST STORMS IN RECENT HISTORY

1925 Tri-state twister ripped through three states of the USA, killing 700 people and injuring more than 2,000.

1951 Tornado killed about 500 people on Comoro Island, off eastern Africa.

1969 Cyclone and resulting floods in Bangladesh killed 500,000 people.

1974 Hurricane Fifi killed 8,000 people in Honduras and left 60,000 people homeless.

1977 20,000 people were killed by a cyclone in southern India.

1979 Hurricane David hit the Caribbean and eastern USA, killing more than 2,000 people.

1984 Typhoon Ike left 1 million people homeless in the Philippines.

1988 Hurricane Gilbert killed 318 people and devastated Jamaica.

1989 Deadliest tornado in history tore through Bangladesh, killing 1,300 people and leaving 50,000 homeless.

1998 Hurricane Mitch killed an estimated 18,000 people in Central America.

2005 Hurricane Katrina killed approximately 1,850 people in the USA.

Prediction and preparation

The only way of reducing the damage and destruction that tornadoes and hurricanes cause is to find more efficient ways of predicting where and when they will happen, and to be better prepared. The path tornadoes will follow is particularly hard to predict so scientists are always exploring new methods of learning more about these storms.

Predicting hurricanes

To learn how fast a hurricane is growing and how fast its winds are blowing, hurricane hunters fly directly into a hurricane in special planes with equipment that can take measurements, including wind speeds and temperature, and photographs of inside the storm. Scientists also study satellite photos to work out which clouds might be potential hurricanes and to track hurricanes after they have formed. Meteorologists in hurricane centres gather weather data from around the world to help them with their predictions.

Storm chasers, such as this team in Kansas, USA, follow tornadoes in fast vehicles to try to get as close to the tornado funnel as they can.

Learning about tornadoes

As well as studying weather patterns and satellite photos as they do for hurricanes, tornado experts also use technology called Doppler radars. These use sound waves to sense the movement and moisture in the air, to work out whether particular strong winds might become a tornado. Experts also use information gathered by storm chasers – scientists who brave danger to follow twisters to record and measure them.

Using results from Doppler radars and reports from trained storm chasers, meteorologists make computer simulations of tornadoes and thunderstorms. It is hoped that this will help them gain a better understanding of these storms and allow them to increase tornado warning times and improve guidelines for building construction.

This new home in Bangladesh has a sturdy concrete base to help it withstand battering from tornadoes and floods. The walls and roof are designed in panels that can be dismantled and put back together after a storm.

Being prepared

Even in poor or remote countries where people do not have easy access to mobile phones, radio or television, there are ways of being better prepared. For example, homes can be redesigned to better resist damage and relocated to higher ground to avoid flood waters. People should be warned about storm dangers if they live in high-risk areas and shown which evacuation routes they should follow. Local people can be trained in first aid and disaster assessment so they can provide immediate assistance after a disaster.

GROWING RISK

Even with improved prediction methods and evacuation plans, many experts believe that the risk of hurricane disasters is still increasing. More and more homes are being built along the world's coastlines. As more people move into the places where hurricanes cause the most damage, these storms are likely to become more destructive.

Glossary

Beaufort scale A scale used to indicate the strength and speed of winds.

climate change The gradual change in long-term weather patterns.

Coriolis Force The force created by the Earth's rotation that causes winds to blow east and west instead of north and south.

debris Scattered material, such as tree branches or building rubble, that has been dislodged or broken and left behind after a hurricane, tornado or other disaster.

delta A fan-shaped area of flat land where a river meets the sea, formed by sediment washed down the river.

displaced When something is moved away from its usual space.

Doppler radar A radar that measures the speed and direction of wind to predict tornadoes.

evacuate To move away from a dangerous place to somewhere safe.

Fujita scale The system used to classify tornadoes according to wind damage.

hurricane seasons The times of the year when hurricanes are most common.

infrastructure Things built for services and communications, such as roads, telephone cables and water pipes.

landslide The sudden movement of a mass of soil and rocks down a slope.

LEDC A less economically developed country (one where average income for people is very low and industry is sparse).

looting The act of stealing from the property of others.

MEDC A more economically developed country (one where average income for people is high and industry is plentiful).

meteorologists Scientists who study and predict the weather.

monsoon A wind that blows across Asia at certain times of year, bringing heavy rains and often causing floods.

radar An instrument that locates objects by beaming radio waves at them and shows the reflected waves on a screen.

sanitation The collection and treatment of waste water.

satellite A scientific object that revolves in space, usually carrying equipment that can transmit signals to and from Earth.

storm cellar An underground shelter where people are safe from a storm.

storm surge A rise in sea level under a storm such as a hurricane, caused by low air pressure and high winds.

supercell A severe thunderstorm with a rotating updraft that can create tornadoes.

Tornado Alley Part of the USA, from Texas to Iowa, where tornadoes often strike.

tropical Relating to the region of Earth on either side of the Equator that is warm and usually humid.

tropical depression A tropical hurricane or cyclone with winds of 62 kph or less.

tropical storm A tropical hurricane or cyclone with winds of up to 120 kph.

typhoon A term used for a hurricane that occurs in regions around the Pacific and Indian oceans (also called a cyclone).

updraft A warm column of air rising in a cloud.

water vapour The gas form of water, produced when water is heated.

Further Information

Books

Awesome Forces of Nature: Howling Hurricanes
Louise and Richard Spilsbury
Heinemann, 2003

Awesome Forces of Nature: Terrifying Tornadoes
Louise and Richard Spilsbury
Heinemann, 2003

DK Eyewitness Guide: Hurricane and Tornado
Jack Challoner
Dorling Kindersley, 2004

Kingfisher Knowledge: Hurricanes, Tsunamis, and Other Natural Disasters
Andrew Langley
Kingfisher, 2006

Websites

www.disasterrelief.org
Type 'tornado' or 'hurricane' into the search box for information about coping with these natural disasters.

www.usgs.gov
Enter 'tornado' or 'hurricane' into the search box for lots of information and links to sites about these destructive winds.

www.fema.gov/kids/tornado.htm
This site tells you about tornado dangers and how to be prepared.

www.tornadochaser.net/educate
Read about and watch videos of tornadoes in the past, learn how to stay safe in a tornado, and make your own twister!

Index